GIFT WRAP REDUX

Vintage Coloring Book

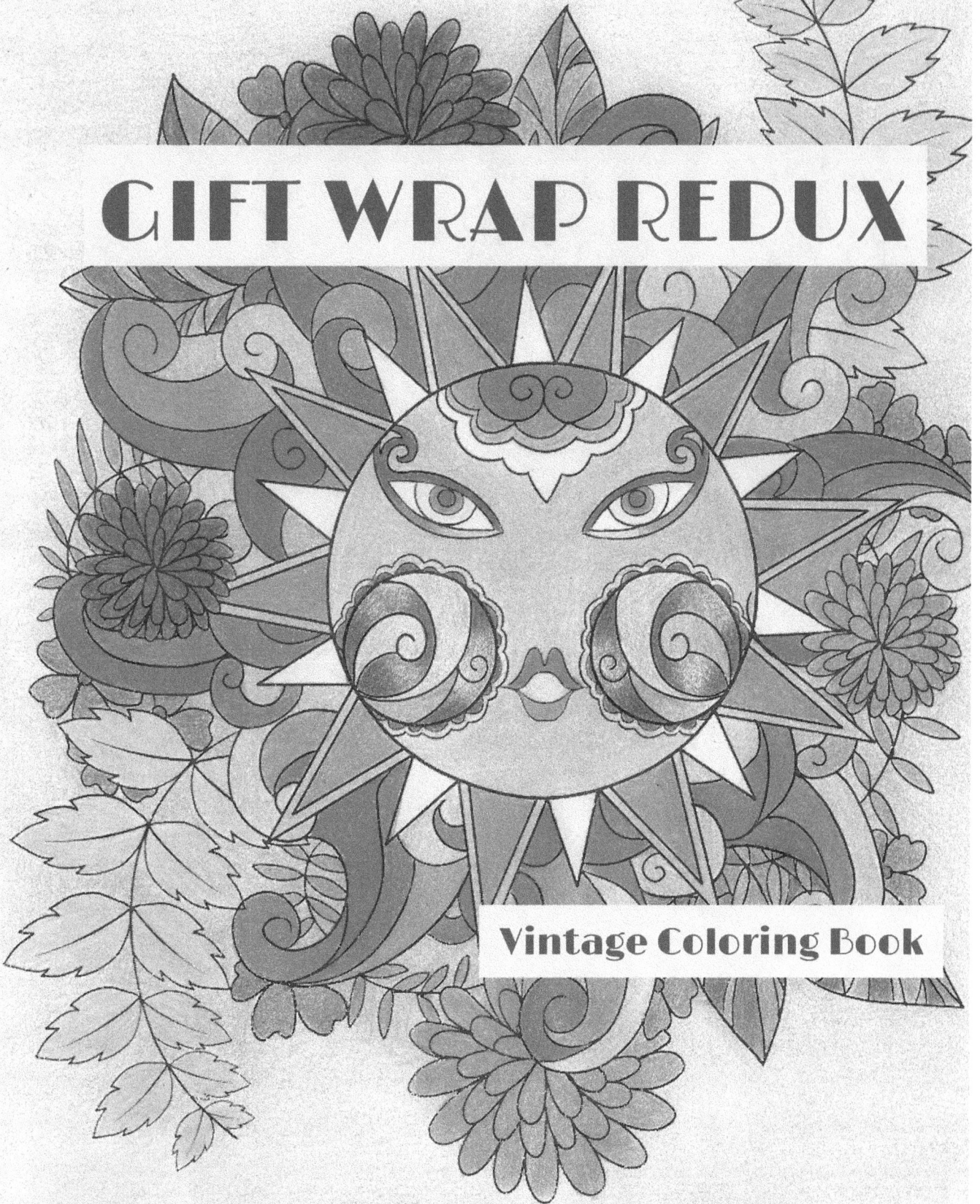

LIGHTBURST
MEDIA

LightBurst Media
www.lightburstmedia.com

Hi.

We are glad you have decided to embark on a coloring adventure with Gift Wrap Redux: Vintage Coloring Book.

It is recommended that you use colored pencils to color the images. If you use another medium, such as markers or gel pens, you can place a blank sheet underneath the page you are coloring. There are extra sheets of paper in the back of the book that you can use for this purpose or to test out color combinations.

We invite you to join our mailing list at lightburstmedia.com. When you join, we will send you five coloring pages from an upcoming coloring book. In addition, you will be the first to receive updates and free coloring pages from our future coloring books.

We would greatly appreciate you leaving an honest review on Amazon for Gift Wrap Redux and sincerely hope that it provides you with many hours of enjoyment, relaxation and fun!

Color Your Dreams,
Bonnie Bright
LightBurst Media

SHOW US YOUR FINISHED COLORING PAGES!

t

f

@lightburstmedia

www.facebook.com/lightburstmedia

lightburstmedia

#lightburstmediacoloring

Send us your completed work and we will proudly share it on our feeds!

You can also email us your feedback, suggestions, completed work, etc.

We love to hear from you.

FEEDBACK@LIGHTBURSTMEDIA.COM

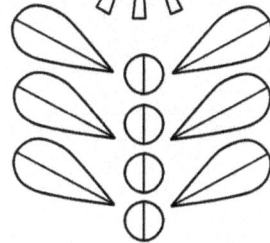

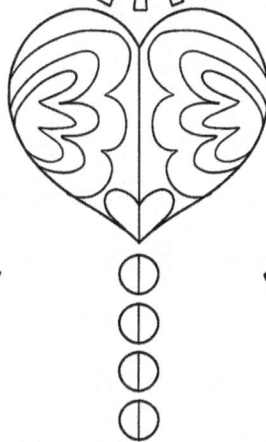

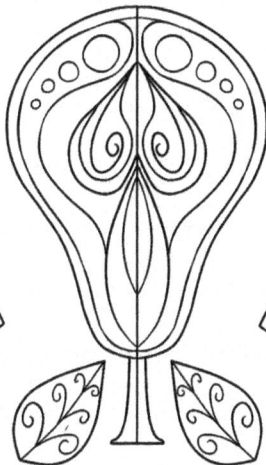

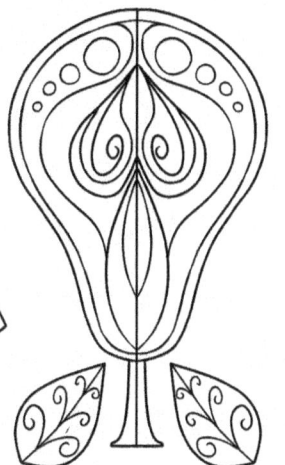

Love Darling

MY DEAR

I
You

BE MY
VALENTINE